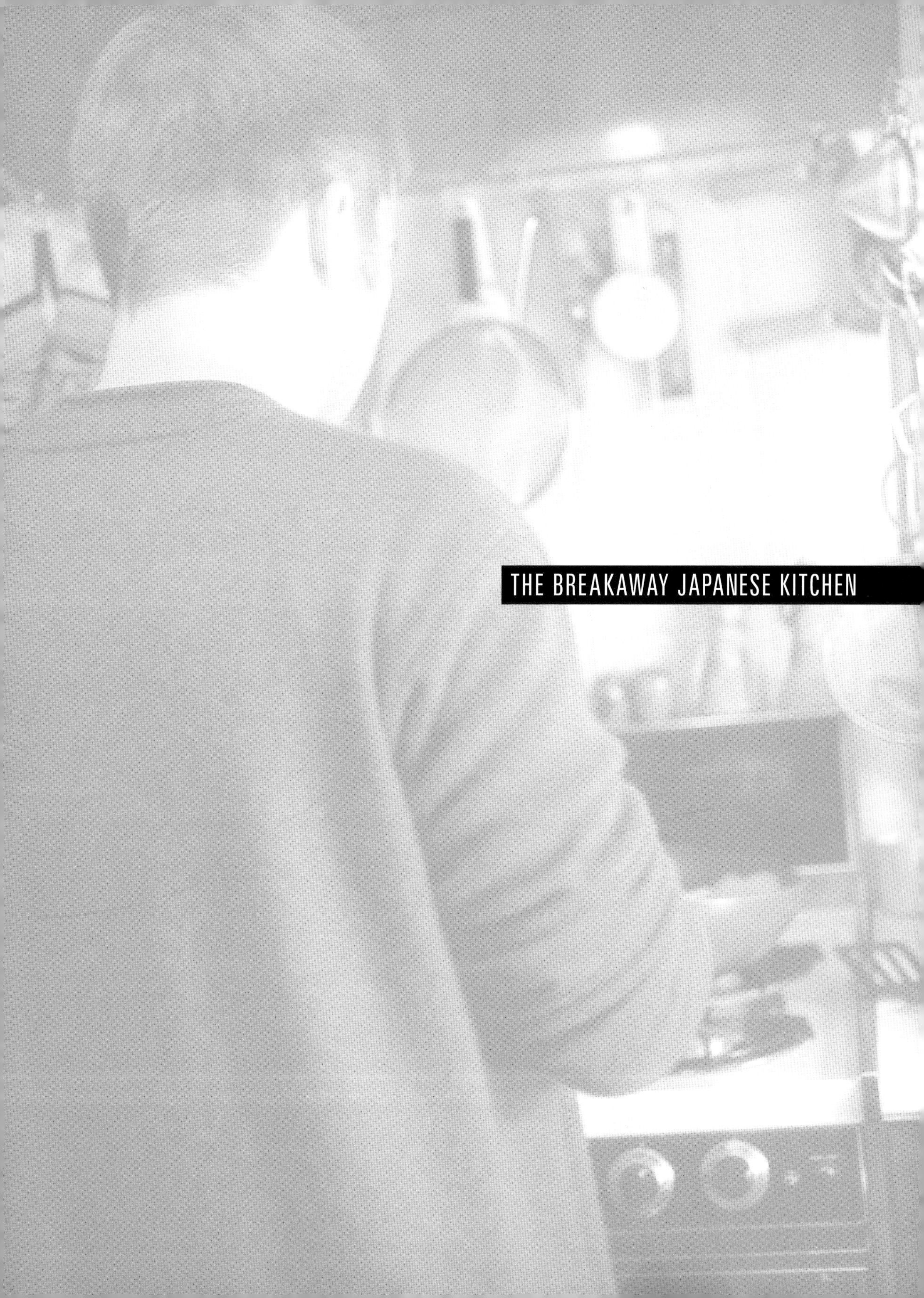

THE BREAKAWAY JAPANESE KITCHEN

Distributed in the United States by Kodansha America, Inc., 575 Lexington Avenue, New York, NY 10022, and in the United Kingdom and continental Europe by Kodansha Europe Ltd., 95 Aldwych, London WC2B 4JF.

Published by Kodansha International Ltd., 17–14 Otowa 1-chome, Bunkyo-ku, Tokyo 112–8652, and Kodansha America, Inc. Copyright © 2003 by Eric Gower.

ISBN 4–7700–2949–7
First edition, 2003
03 04 05 06 07 08 09 10   10 9 8 7 6 5 4 3 2 1

Library of Congress Cataloging-in-Publication Data available

www.thejapanpage.com

THE BREAKAWAY JAPANESE KITCHEN

INSPIRED NEW TASTES

ERIC GOWER

PHOTOGRAPHS BY FUMIHIKO WATANABE

KODANSHA INTERNATIONAL
Tokyo•New York•London

CONTENTS

INTRODUCTION

One of the best things about living in a country that has a great culinary tradition is that you get to eat a hell of a lot of good food. My 15-year stay in Japan has exposed me to some of the most delightful gastronomy on the planet. It's reassuring, to put it mildly, to know that I can walk outside and eat world-class meals any time I like. I feel blessed to have been surrounded with so much good, authentic Japanese food and ingredients for so long. The country is a cook's paradise.

I started experimenting with Japanese cuisine and ingredients because, after having a great many first-rate but orthodox meals, I discovered it was fun to push the boundaries a bit. I still like to reproduce Japanese classics, but what I enjoy doing most in my own kitchen is delighting my own senses, incorporating ingredients and techniques that may stray a bit from the traditional but that really do it for me. And that is what cooking is really about: making things that delight you. You will almost certainly find that your enthusiasm becomes infectious, and that others will enjoy the results too.

I think that most people who really enjoy going out for Japanese food have been reluctant to delve into experimenting with it on their own because it just seems too daunting. But it should be recalled that French cuisine, marvelous as it is, was stuck in a traditional rut before a whole new generation of chefs started borrowing and incorporating and fusing, often with exhilarating results. California cuisine has always been about the attraction of disparate elements; while this was less successful in the early days, with the new emphasis on the hyperlocal and the hyper-fresh, it is now spawning some of the most innovative and delicious food around.

There's no reason a similar revolution can't happen with Japanese cuisine. But we first have to break free of the idea that food has to be traditional to be taken seriously.

One day shortly after arriving in Kyoto, I was taken by a friend to a traditional kaiseki restaurant—which involves umpteen courses of seasonal cuisine in teeny portions, all in a tightly defined order and served on sumptuous pottery. It was a real eye-opener because of the amount of care, time, and resources that could be put into something like lunch. It never really inspired me to try to incorporate kaiseki-style food as part of my daily life, but sitting in a pleasant room and having someone bring you up to twenty courses of some of the world's tastiest morsels, all the while sipping premium sake and tea, is a wonderful way to spend the day.

That is tradition at its best, and it's impossible to overemphasize how delicious traditional

Japanese cuisine is. Time-honored (and we're talking centuries here) traditions got to be the way they are because some inherent balance was struck, the results were great and relatively easily reproducible, and people simply passed on their knowledge and experience. The cuisines of all regions throughout the world follow this pattern.

But tradition can get a little fetishized, and this is especially true in Japan. There is great reverence for the way things have always been done. That same emphasis on tradition is precisely what appeals to many non-Japanese. Think of Japan, and it's hard not to imagine its temples, its ancient but extremely modern sense of clean, minimalist design, and its gorgeous, artful food.

Happily, young Japanese chefs today—almost certainly influenced by their many trips abroad—are branching out. After developing sound foundations they are using them as springboards for innovation. Yet even more Japanese cooks seem to believe that experimentation is for the unserious. In other words, it's fine if you're bored and want to play around a little, but you prove your worth as a cook by flawlessly executing the classics, at least for a while. And of course the sensei, or expert, or whoever it is that knows more than you do, has to give his seal of approval on everything. Many Japanese chefs take it as a given that palate—to my mind, the *only* measure of a meal's worth—is a secondary consideration.

And it isn't just chefs. Ordinary Japanese, like people everywhere, come to like and expect the standard repertoire when it comes to Japanese food. They learn from childhood that there's a right way to eat almost anything. Tonkatsu (fried pork cutlets) is served with tonkatsu sweet sauce, always. Pickled ginger goes with sushi. Fresh tofu gets soy sauce, ginger, and chopped green onions. You dip zaru-soba (cold buckwheat noodles) in tsuyu (a kind of dipping sauce), and only tsuyu. Edamame are shucked and popped with beer as snacks. People everywhere, of course, do this—vinegar with the chips in England, ketchup for the fries in the US, mayo for the frites in Belgium—but not to the same extent.

Rice, moreover, is sacred in Japan, and is simply not messed with at all. Rice is a deeply embedded cultural concept, used in countless ceremonies and rituals, many of which involve the emperor and the imperial family. Moreover, rice means *japonica*, and no other. Back around 1992, Japan's rice industry had a horrible harvest, and Thai rice had to be imported in large quantities, producing a massive outpouring of protest from Japanese housewives. My local rice seller used to give me as many five-kilogram bags of it as I could carry, for free; there simply wasn't a market for it, and much of it, sadly, wound up in dumpsters. No other kind of rice is available in stores, unless you count the little $12 half-pound bags of Minnesota wild rice at my local gourmet store.

■　■　■

Outsiders, like me, who weren't exposed to any of that conditioning, are by definition freer than the average Japanese regarding the preparation of food. I love, for example, to brush a mixture of umeboshi (super-sour pickled plums), olive oil, some apricot jam, and some shallots over a nice piece of young yellowtail, and broil it. I also like to combine pickled ginger (usually eaten between pieces of sushi), fresh figs (dessert), and extra virgin olive oil (Italian), and spoon it over creamy tofu (Japanese)—a truly delicious combination that unfortunately tends to freak Japanese people out. Until they try it. My favorite thing to do with edamame is to purée a little with some olive oil and fresh shiso leaves, and to add fruit—the big meaty Bing cherries work beautifully here—then mix this sauce in with the rest of the edamame, and eat it with smoked salmon and a bone-dry chilled white wine. It's a beautiful dish, and most people really like it, but it's just a heart-stopper for most Japanese.

As you gain confidence as a cook, you'll cook more often, and become more flexible and improvisational. Or at least that's what happened to me. I never went to cooking school or cooked in a restaurant—I learned by cooking thousands of meals, many of them without adequate time, planning, or even cookware. I use little more than a couple of good pots and pans, an old oven I bought for 3,000 yen ($25) from a neighbor, an excellent blender, and a few sharp knives. I do try to keep a fairly well-stocked pantry because I realize that I often don't feel like shopping for fresh ingredients. I know I can make dozens of healthy, tasty meals just by always having a good supply of pasta, dried and fresh fruits, nuts, fresh herbs, eggs, onions, garlic, lemons, tofu, potatoes, excellent olive oils, and several kinds of vinegar (okay, about 15 kinds of vinegar).

What I always try to do is make use of everyday Japanese ingredients in new and accessible ways, while remaining grounded in sound culinary principles. Novelty for novelty's sake has not—at least I hope—played any kind of role in these pages.

A great part of the joy in cooking for me is spontaneity. Almost anything can be interchanged at will, depending on mood and what is available. It's okay to use lamb instead of beef, or tofu instead of chicken, or to just omit the protein altogether. Any degree of acidity can be added through the use of citrus or vinegar (whose heavy use in these pages tips you off to my preference), or any intensity of heat through the use of chiles. Herbs can be freely exchanged. You can use more or less intense heat than called for. The only "right" way to cook something is to make it exactly how you enjoy it most. Cooking doesn't have to be complicated to be interesting, unusual, and delicious. And it certainly doesn't have to be arduous, as I've tried to demonstrate here.

And finally, contrary to popular opinion, wine actually goes marvelously well with Japanese-inspired dishes. Most of the dishes presented here have been created from the start to be served with wine, and come with specific varietal suggestions for pairing. For me, drinking wine with a meal vastly enhances the flavor of the food and the pleasure of eating it. It can't be a fluke that in two of the world's greatest cuisines, those of Italy and France, it would be almost unthinkable to serve meals without wine. Wine is simply part of the equation. In traditional settings Japanese food is not paired with wine, but I hope you'll agree with me in thinking that the combinations suggested here are mutually enhancing.

A person's approach to food is a good barometer of the way they approach life in general. I hope to inspire home cooks who want to expand their repertoire, to enjoy the process more, and to cook great food without impossible amounts of time or hassle.

Seafood

Many Japanese believe that the best way to enjoy fresh fish is to eat it raw. Part of me shares this belief, but part doesn't. There is no doubt that eating fish sashimi-style is the best way to actually taste the fish, especially at a top-class sushi restaurant. But at home, there are times when I want to eat my fish with flavor other than wasabi and soy sauce; I like to grill it, pan-fry it, and roast it. These methods are extremely simple, take almost no time, and are mastered easily.

Fortunately, most American and European home cooks today are blessed with a good selection of fresh fish. It seems obvious to say, but, as with vegetables, you should buy whatever looks best that day, even if you were planning on cooking something else. It's better to substitute, or change recipes altogether, than to use an inferior piece of fish.

Most of the fish dishes here can be made in less than 10 minutes. Serve them to guests—people will think you spent half your day in the kitchen and the food will spark great conversation.

Ceviche Japonesa

This tart dish is the definition of versatile; you can substitute any firm-fleshed white fish for the scallops, and substitute almost anything for the vegetables and fruit, allowing you maximum flexibility according to what's available each season. I like to use persimmons when I can get them, and avocado when I can't, but it's also great with Asian pear or any of the big tropical fruits. It's best to let the ceviche sit for 5 or 10 minutes before serving, which allows the lime juice to slightly "cook" the scallops. Champagne is the drink of choice here.

■ ■ ■

SERVES 4

about 10 large very fresh scallops (sashimi grade)

1 avocado, peeled and diced

¼ bell pepper (red, orange, or yellow), minced

2 tablespoons baby ginger, minced

2 tablespoons red onion, minced

juice of 1 lime

several tablespoons light soy sauce (to taste)

1 tablespoon fruity extra virgin olive oil

sea salt

fresh coarsely ground black pepper

1 tablespoon maple syrup, if needed (taste the dish first, and add only if it's too tart)

zest of 1 lime, minced

2 tablespoons chives, minced

Slice the scallops into small pieces and place in a large bowl. Gently mix in the avocado, bell pepper, baby ginger, and red onion. Add the lime juice, soy sauce, and olive oil, and season with salt and pepper. Mix, taste for sweetness, and add the maple syrup only if it seems too tart. Spoon into individual bowls, and top with the zest and then the chives.

The formula here is "savory, sweet, boozy." You can substitute anything savory for the miso (last night's leftover pasta sauce, say), anything for the sweet, such as maple syrup or puréed fruit, and anything for the sake, such as leftover wine or even brandy. As always, keep experimenting!

White Fish with Shallots and Miso Apricot Glaze

Any firm-fleshed white fish will work here—rock cod, sea bass, orange roughy, even catfish. The glaze—miso plus sweetened fruit—is in the style of Kyoto cuisine, and goes exceedingly well with a flask of chilled premium sake.

■   ■   ■

SERVES 2

1 teaspoon light miso

1 teaspoon apricot jam

2 tablespoons sake

1 tablespoon extra virgin olive oil

2 fillets white fish, about $\frac{1}{2}$ pound (225 gr) total

fresh coarsely ground black pepper

2 tablespoons shallots, minced

Mix the miso, jam, and sake together in a cup. Turn on the broiler. Rub the oil on the fillets, pepper them, and place in a broiling pan. Broil for about 2 minutes, spoon on some of the sauce, and sprinkle on the shallots. Broil until browned, about 3 minutes. Depending on what kind of fish you use, you may need to turn it over, spoon on more sauce, and broil the other side. Serve on warm plates.

Salmon Tartare with Shiso

I only recently discovered the delightfulness of the combination of sashimi-grade salmon, good olive oil, and shiso. At the end of the shiso season, the bolting plant releases hundreds of seeds, which are also marvelous in the recipe, giving it a satisfying little crunch. If you can't find shiso leaves or seeds, the recipe also works beautifully with tarragon, though it will change its character away from the minty direction of the shiso and toward anise.

■ ■ ■

SERVES 3 OR 4 AS A STARTER

about 1/4 pound (110 gr) of the best sashimi-grade salmon you can find

1 tablespoon extra virgin olive oil, plus additional for dressing the greens

2 tablespoons rice vinegar, plus additional for dressing the greens

sea salt

fresh coarsely ground black pepper

1 tablespoon minced shiso

1 tablespoon shiso, chiffonade

handful of arugula, torn into small pieces

Slice the salmon thinly and then roughly chop up the slices (it's nice to have lots of differently sized pieces). Put the fish in a bowl and add the olive oil, vinegar, salt, and pepper, and mix. Add the minced shiso and mix. Taste for salt.

On four small plates arrange the arugula in a ring. Lightly dress the greens with oil and vinegar, and dust them with salt and pepper. Spoon the salmon into the center, and top with the shiso chiffonade. A bone-dry, grassy sauvignon blanc from New Zealand is a winner with this dish.

Hamachi Tataki with Tomato-Ginger Sauce

"Tataki" refers to a Japanese technique that sears the outside of fish and meats over very high heat, and leaves the middle uncooked. The texture of the rare and the seared fish together is delightful, and is accented further by the piquancy of the tomato-ginger blend. A chilled glass of viognier is a nice accompaniment.

■ ■ ■

SERVES 2

1 medium tomato

1 tablespoon light soy sauce

1 tablespoon butter

2 tablespoons extra virgin olive oil

2 tablespoons shallots, chopped

1 tablespoon fresh ginger, diced

sea salt

fresh coarsely ground black pepper

sashimi-grade yellowtail, about $\frac{1}{3}$ pound (150 gr)

daikon sprouts or other sprouts, optional

Boil some water in a saucepan and blanch the tomato for about a minute, until the skin loosens. Rinse under cold water, remove the skin and seeds, and put in a blender. Add the soy sauce and blend. In a small sauté pan heat the butter and 1 tablespoon of the olive oil, add the shallots and ginger, salt and pepper them, and sauté for about 5 minutes over low heat. Add to the blender, blend with the tomato, and return the mixture to the pan. Simmer on very low heat for about 5 minutes, while you do the next step.

Heat the other tablespoon of oil in a heavy skillet over maximum heat until very hot, and sear both sides of the yellowtail. Be careful not to overcook it. Remove to a chopping board, and carefully slice it into bite-sized portions. Spoon a little of the sauce onto a heated plate and place the fish in it. Spoon more sauce over and top with the optional sprouts.

Scallops with Miso, Ginger, and Ruby Grapefruit

Miso and citrus is a classic Japanese combination. But here instead of the traditional Japanese citrus, yuzu, I use ruby grapefruit. The fusion of the scallops, sauce, and grapefruit sections somehow produces a whole that is so much more than the sum of its parts. A chilled premium sake, or almost any good white table wine, just intensifies the effect.

■　■　■

SERVES 2 OR 3

1 tablespoon butter

2 tablespoons minced shallots

2 tablespoons fresh ginger, minced

sea salt

fresh coarsely ground black pepper

juice of 1/2 ruby grapefruit

1 tablespoon light miso

1 tablespoon rice vinegar

1 tablespoon sake

1 tablespoon flour

1 tablespoon fresh thyme, chopped

2 tablespoons fresh oregano, chopped

1/2 pound (225 gr) very fresh scallops

2 tablespoons extra virgin olive oil

1/4 cup radicchio, roughly chopped

1/2 fresh ruby grapefruit, sectioned and all tough skin removed

1 tablespoon chives, minced

Heat the butter in a nonstick skillet, add the shallots, ginger, salt, and pepper, and sauté over low heat for about 5 minutes. Put the grapefruit juice, miso, vinegar, and sake in a blender, and blend. When the shallots begin to soften, add this mixture to the pan and simmer, until the volume is reduced by about three-fourths.

Meanwhile, toss the flour, thyme, and oregano together in a bowl. Salt and pepper to taste, mix, and then add the scallops, coating them well. In another large skillet heat the oil over high heat, and sear the scallops on both sides, turning just once, until they are firm and lightly golden. On a warm plate, scatter the radicchio, place the scallops on it, and arrange some of the grapefruit sections however you like. Add the sauce to the skillet in which you cooked the scallops, deglazing it and scraping up the brown bits. Carefully spoon over the scallops and grapefruit, and top with the chives.

Littleneck Clams with Umeboshi Broth

Umeboshi (pickled plums) are traditionally eaten after a meal—many Japanese feel that they aid digestion—but here we're using them for their salty-sour intensity to make a lovely broth. You can usually find an assortment of umeboshi in any Asian market.

■　■　■

SERVES 2

1 tablespoon butter

2 tablespoons shallots, minced

½ cup sake

10 large meaty umeboshi, pitted

½ cup carrot juice

1 tablespoon soy sauce

1 pound (450 gr) littleneck clams, rinsed

1 tablespoon chives or cilantro, optional

Heat the butter in a small skillet and sauté the shallots for about 5 minutes, until soft. In a blender mix the sake, umeboshi, carrot juice, soy sauce, and sautéed shallots. Place the mixture in a skillet large enough to hold the clams, bring to a boil, add the clams, cover, and simmer until the clams open, about 5 minutes. Serve in large heated bowls, topping off with the optional chives or cilantro.

Crab with Lime Ponzu and Chipotle

Most Japanese stocks start with the addition of konbu, a savory seaweed widely available in Asian markets. In this version we add piquancy from the lime and heat and smokiness from the chipotle. Also works beautifully with yuzu, Japanese citrus, if you're lucky enough to find it. I like a dry riesling with this.

■ ■ ■

SERVES 2 AS A STARTER

¼ cup water

2 tablespoons sake

2 tablespoons soy sauce

1 stick dried konbu

zest of 1 lime, minced

juice of 1 lime

small pinch chipotle (or other chili powder)

¼ pound (110 gr) fresh cooked Dungeness
    (or other) crabmeat

Bring the water to a boil in a small saucepan, add everything but the crab, and simmer for about 20 minutes, until the liquid is reduced by about half. Discard the konbu, pour the mixture into a small bowl, and use as a dipping sauce for the crab.

Salads

Salads are really more about shopping than cooking, as the freshness of the ingredients take center stage. Fortunately for most people today, farmers' markets are everywhere, and you can easily pick up hyperfresh, gorgeous, and local produce for modest prices.

The increasing availability of edamame, shiso, kabocha, and persimmons even in mainstream supermarkets means that the salads included here can be made easily and regularly.

These salads are substantial enough to be considered an equal component, along with an entrée and perhaps a grain, of any meal. With a good crusty bread and a decent bottle of wine, they can also be the main dish.

Japanese Coleslaw

This 5-minute salad really energizes, especially if all the ingredients are well chilled as you begin. In just a few minutes you have a healthy and satisfying component of a meal. Goes well with grilled fish.

■   ■   ■

SERVES 3 OR 4

2 cups shredded green cabbage

2 cups shredded red cabbage

1 large carrot, grated

2 tablespoons walnut oil (or other light, neutral oil)

1 teaspoon sesame oil

2 tablespoons brown rice vinegar

1 tablespoon light soy sauce

1 tablespoon maple syrup, or honey

2 tablespoons freshly grated ginger

$1/4$ cup finely chopped peanuts

Combine the cabbages and carrot in a large bowl. Toss with your hands and set aside. To make the dressing, combine the walnut oil, sesame oil, vinegar, soy sauce, maple syrup, and ginger in a small bowl, and whisk. Pour over the salad and toss well. Sprinkle on the peanuts.

Kabocha Salad

This attractive and colorful dish is good year-round. It makes a fine meal with a cup of soup and some crusty bread. You can substitute almost any kind of squash for the kabocha.

■ ■ ■

4 tablespoons extra virgin olive oil

1/2 medium kabocha, skin removed, cut into bite-sized cubes, 3 ounces (90 gr)

fresh coarsely ground black pepper

1/2 cup carrot juice

1 tablespoon soy sauce

1 tablespoon nam pla (Thai fish sauce)

6 strips thick bacon

1 cup red cabbage, thinly sliced

2 tablespoons fresh cilantro (or parsley), chopped

In a large nonstick skillet, heat up 3 tablespoons of the olive oil over high heat, and add the kabocha. Coat all pieces well, and liberally pepper. Lower the flame a little, and sauté them for about 5 minutes, stirring constantly. Add the carrot juice, bring to a boil, cover, and turn down the heat very low. Cook about 10 minutes, until the liquid disappears. Transfer to a large bowl and add the soy sauce, nam pla, and the remaining tablespoon of oil, and mix gently but thoroughly. In another small frying pan, quickly cook the bacon over medium-high heat, until browned and crispy. Make a bed of the cabbage on a plate, and spoon on some kabocha. Chop up the bacon, and sprinkle it over the kabocha. Top with the cilantro.

If you're using packaged, shelled edamame, microwave or boil them briefly, according to instructions. If you're using uncooked edamame in their shells, boil them about 5 minutes over a medium flame, rinse with cold water, and shell.

Smoked Salmon with Edamame, Cherry, and Shiso

This filling yet light dish is a visual feast—it's a lovely first course for just about any dinner menu. You can substitute a blood orange for the cherries, with marvelous effect.

■ ■ ■

SERVES 3 OR 4 AS A STARTER, OR 2 AS A MAIN

1 cup edamame, cooked and shelled

10 or so fresh shiso leaves, 1 reserved and sliced thinly

3 tablespoons extra virgin olive oil

8–10 large Bing cherries or other cherries, pitted and chopped, plus a few extra for garnish

1 tablespoon rice vinegar

sea salt

fresh coarsely ground black pepper

smoked salmon, 2 ounces (60 gr)

Put the shiso, olive oil, cherries, vinegar, salt, pepper, and 2 tablespoons of the shelled edamame in a blender and blend. Add this to the remaining edamame and mix. On a large plate, layer the salmon in a circle, and spoon the mixture over it, using the extra cherries and reserved shiso as garnish. Adjust the salt.

Beet Salad with Ginger, Smoked Trout, and Walnuts

Vibrant, freshly cooked beets bear no resemblance to the canned monstrosities we all hated as children. This colorful salad can be a meal in itself if you have a nice loaf of crusty bread around. Nice with an Australian semillon white blend.

■　■　■

SERVES 3 OR 4

2 cups cooked beets (2 to 3 medium beets)	2 tablespoons rice vinegar (or other vinegar)
1 cup cooked beet greens (or other winter greens)	2 tablespoons orange juice
	sea salt
2 tablespoons ginger, minced	fresh coarsely ground black pepper
1 tablespoon shallots, minced	¼ pound (110 gr) smoked trout
3 tablespoons extra virgin olive oil	2 tablespoons walnuts, chopped

Set a pot of water to boil. Cut the beets from their stems. Remove the leaves from their tough backbone stems, rinse well, and set aside. Boil the beets for about 40 minutes over low heat, until tender. While they're cooking, sauté the ginger and shallots in 1 tablespoon of the olive oil for about 5 minutes, until soft.

Remove the cooked beets with a slotted spoon, rinse under cold water, and slip off the skins. Cut the beets into small pieces, and place in a bowl. Add another tablespoon of the olive oil, 1 tablespoon of the vinegar, the ginger-shallot mixture, the orange juice, and salt and pepper to taste. Boil the leaves in the hot red water for a few minutes, remove and rinse, and squeeze out as much water as you can. Chop them up and drizzle on the remaining tablespoon of the olive oil and tablespoon of the vinegar.

Place the leaves in the center of a large plate, and surround with the beets (or mix the leaves and beets together if you think it looks better). Scatter the trout all around. Toast the walnuts for a few minutes in a dry skillet and top the salad with them.

Persimmon Yogurt Salad with Ginger, Red Onion, and Mint

This dish is, I suppose, a kind of fruity raita. Especially good when served with something spicy.

■ ■ ■

SERVES 2 OR 3

1 tablespoon fresh ginger, minced

2 tablespoons red onion, minced

1 large Fuyu persimmon, sliced thin

3 tablespoons plain yogurt

2 tablespoons fresh mint, chopped

1 tablespoon soy sauce

fresh coarsely ground black pepper

Heat a small pot of water to boil, blanch the ginger and onion for about a minute, and drain. Combine all the other ingredients in a large bowl, add the ginger and onion, and gently mix. Keep well chilled.

Tofu

This section, alas, comes with a big disclaimer: it's tough to find really tasty tofu outside Japan. I much prefer the creamy tofu known as *oborodofu*, which probably resembles custard more than it does even the softest tofu available in the United States or Europe, known as "silken" tofu. By all means use this creamy version if you can find it, but you may have to make do with the silken variety. Medium, firm, and—god forbid—extra-firm tofu should be avoided for the recipes presented here.

Tofu is cheap, has almost no fat or calories, and is very versatile—it absorbs whatever flavors you care to impart on it. I almost always keep a tub of it around for a quick, tasty, healthy meal.

Because none of the recipes that follow are traditional, my Japanese friends always express surprise at the techniques and flavors. Tofu, I think, has a long way to go in overcoming the unfortunate reputation it earned as the tasteless cardboard gum served up earnestly by many well-meaning folks in the 1970s. Let's hope these recipes change at least a few minds!

One word on preparation: always drain it well. We want as much water as possible removed from it. I usually remove it from the package, discard the soaking water, gently press it between my hands, and then wrap a paper towel or two around it until I'm ready to use it.

Shiso Tofu

This is a kind of wafu (Japanese-style) pesto, except that it's spooned over fresh soft tofu, not pasta. This dish really wakes up the palate and the appetite, so it's good to serve it as the first course of a special meal.

■   ■   ■

SERVES 2 OR 3

20 fresh shiso leaves

1 heaping tablespoon baby ginger, minced (normal ginger will work too)

zest of 1 orange (or other orange citrus), 1 tablespoon reserved

3 to 4 tablespoons juice of any orange citrus

1 tablespoon extra virgin olive oil

1 tablespoon brown rice vinegar (or other vinegar)

sea salt

fresh coarsely ground black pepper

1 tub oborodofu, about ½ pound (200–250 gr)

Blend everything except the tofu in the blender. Divide the tofu into two or three of your prettiest bowls, and spoon over the sauce. Taste for salt, and garnish with the reserved zest.

Citrus zest adds a tremendous boost of flavor and complexity to whatever it touches, has virtually no calories, and costs almost nothing. I can't get enough of it. A ten-dollar investment in a Microplane zester will reward you for years, but you certainly don't need one. Just slice off the peel of any citrus with a veg-etable peeler or sharp knife, scrape away any bitter white pith clinging to it, and mince it up.

Tofu Mushroom "Casserole"

At first glance this dish may look complicated, but the whole thing can be put together in about 10 minutes. And with only 20 minutes of oven time, you're eating half an hour after you start prepping. A unique and wonderful thing to do with tofu. I like a glass of zinfandel with this.

■ ■ ■

SERVES 2 OR 3

3 tablespoons extra virgin olive oil

3 cups mushrooms (any kind; a mixture is nice), chopped

fresh coarsely ground black pepper

½ cup bell pepper (any color, or better, a combination of colors), chopped

2 tablespoons gari (pickled ginger)

3 tablespoons light soy sauce

1 block silken tofu, about ½ pound (200–250 gr)

1 egg

3 tablespoons minced green onions

1 tablespoon minced Italian parsley, optional

All tofu should be well drained before using. The tried-and-true method is to set it between two cutting boards that are slanted toward the sink, and wait for about an hour. But I'm often too impatient and just squeeze it gently between my hands, then dry it well with a paper towel. You may get a little residual water in the tofu casserole when done. Just drain it and ignore it; it won't affect anything.

Preheat the oven to 400°F (200°C). Heat 2 tablespoons of the oil in a heavy skillet and add the mushrooms. Liberally pepper them and sauté on medium heat for about 5 minutes. While they're cooking, put the bell pepper, gari, 2 tablespoons of the soy sauce, and 1 tablespoon of the olive oil in the blender and blend. Add this mixture to the mushrooms and continue cooking another few minutes, until most of the liquid disappears.

Rinse out the blender and blend together the tofu, egg, green onions, the remaining tablespoon of soy sauce, and black pepper.

Lightly oil a medium-sized ceramic or glass baking dish, and pour the mixture from the blender into it. Fold in the mushroom mixture, and sprinkle some more pepper over. Bake for about 20 minutes, until nicely browned on top, slice into wedges, and serve in warm bowls. Taste for salt, and top with the Italian parsley.

FOR INSTRUCTIONS ON MAKING GARI, SEE PAGE 109.

Traditionally eaten in between bites of sushi, pickled ginger is a marvelous palate cleanser. But I often use it in cooking too, in place of regular fresh ginger, when I want even more piquancy.

Tofu with Figs and Pickled Ginger

It's essential to use the softest, freshest tofu you can find here. It works best with fresh figs, but if they're not in season the dried ones are a fine substitute. The pickled ginger can be found in any Asian supermarket. It's also very easy to make yourself, with lots of variations.

■ ■ ■

SERVES 3 OR 4 AS A STARTER (OR 1, IN MY CASE, FOR LUNCH)

3 fresh figs or 2 large (golf ball–sized) dried figs	fresh coarsely ground black pepper
2 heaping tablespoons gari (pickled ginger)	1 tub very fresh tofu, about $\frac{1}{2}$ pound (200–250 gr)
3 tablespoons extra virgin olive oil	1 tablespoon chives, minced finely
sea salt	

Remove the skins from the fresh figs or, if using dried, reconstitute 10 minutes in a small cup of boiled water and trim the ends. Mix all the ingredients except the tofu and chives in a blender. Spoon the sauce over the tofu in a bowl, taste for salt, and top with the chives. May also be microwaved for a minute or two, if you prefer it hot.

FOR INSTRUCTIONS ON MAKING GARI, SEE PAGE **109.**

Tofu Salmon Mousse

This dish is excellent uncooked and cold, as a spread for toasted sourdough bread, and great with a glass of unoaked chardonnay. Or you can briefly cook in the microwave (about 2 minutes) if you prefer a "fluffier" version. Takes a maximum of 5 minutes to prepare. Makes wonderful picnic or brunch food.

■   ■   ■

SERVES 3 OR 4 AS AN APPETIZER

1 loaf very fresh sourdough bread (or
    French baguette)
1 tub oborodofu, about ½ pound (200–
    250 gr)
¼ pound (110 gr) smoked salmon
handful of very fresh walnuts (maybe 2 or
    3 tablespoons)

zest of 1 orange (or clementine, or tanger-
    ine), 1 tablespoon reserved for garnish
2 tablespoons extra virgin olive oil
sea salt
fresh coarsely ground black pepper

Slice the bread very thinly, toast it lightly, and set aside. Blend all the other ingredients together in a blender and taste for salt. Place the mixture in a serving dish or individual dishes. Top with the reserved zest, and spread on the toasted bread.

Baked Tofu with Pistachio and Mint

Another pesto-like creation that people seem to love. Served with a cup of soup and a salad, makes a casual and delightful light meal. A pinot noir stands up to this dish well.

■ ■ ■

SERVES 3 OR 4 AS PART OF ANY MEAL

1 tub oborodofu, about ½ pound (200–250 gr)

½ cup pistachios, shelled

1 cup mint, chopped, 1 tablespoon reserved for
    garnish

⅓ cup extra virgin olive oil

sea salt

fresh coarsely ground black pepper

Preheat the oven to 400°F (200°C). Drain the tofu well, and in a blender mix together all the other ingredients (leaving some of the pistachios in larger chunks, if possible). In a glass or ceramic baking dish, break up the tofu gently with your fingers, and spoon on the sauce. Bake about 20 to 25 minutes, and serve hot in warmed bowls. Taste for salt, and top with the extra mint.

Pasta and Udon

Good udon—and it's often worth buying the slightly more expensive version in Asian grocery stores—has a chewy texture that I love. As in many facets of traditional Japanese cuisine, there is a standard repertoire of udon dishes, and I am very freely taking leave of tradition with these recipes. I opt for pesto-like sauces, as opposed to the customary steaming broths.

With pasta, I try to place a heavy emphasis on Japanese ingredients, which gives the dishes a new spin. Fresh pasta is pretty widely available these days, though a well-stocked pantry full of all kinds of dried pasta is like great meal insurance: you know that a tasty repast is never beyond your reach.

Shiitake Pesto

This earthy, caloric pasta is good on a cold day. Dried shiitake in Japan are almost always reconstituted with hot water and used for flavoring, so this dish never fails to surprise my Japanese friends. Break out a big bordeaux or shiraz for this. Prep time, again, is less than it takes to boil a pot of water for the pasta.

■ ■ ■

SERVES 2 OR 3

10 or 12 medium-large dried shiitake mushrooms

¼ cup smoked or roasted almonds

1 tablespoon cream cheese

1 clove very fresh garlic, chopped (omit if the garlic isn't superfresh)

⅓ cup extra virgin olive oil

coarse salt

fresh coarsely ground black pepper

several tablespoons carrot juice or stock or pasta water, if needed

pasta for 2, about ½ pound (225 gr)

Parmesan cheese (optional)

Set a large pot of salted water to boil for the pasta. Put the mushrooms in the blender and blend until you have a powder. Add the almonds, cream cheese, garlic, and olive oil. Liberally salt and pepper the mixture, and blend. You may need to add some liquid (carrot juice works well here, giving the dish an even bigger, more complex flavor) to make the blender whir. Taste again for salt.

Cook the pasta, drain it, return it to the pot, and mix in the pesto. Taste for salt, and liberally pepper. Top with the optional Parmesan (it's pretty rich as is). Good with a crusty white bread and a mixed green salad.

Edamame Mint Pesto

The skyrocketing popularity of edamame means that they're much easier to find than they used to be. The earthiness of the soybeans combined with the mint produces a delightful lightness that seems designed for a very young, dry white wine like a New Zealand sauvignon blanc. If you can buy frozen edamame that are already shelled—perfectly acceptable for this dish—you'll be eating a few minutes after the pasta water boils.

■ ■ ■

SERVES 2

1 cup edamame, cooked and shelled

¼ cup smoked almonds, cashews, or pine nuts

1 cup fresh mint leaves, chopped, 1 tablespoon reserved

1 clove ultrafresh garlic, peeled

½ cup fruity extra virgin olive oil

sea salt

fresh coarsely ground black pepper

pasta for 2, about ½ pound (225 gr)

Set a large pot of salted water to boil for the pasta. Combine the edamame with everything else (except the pasta) in a blender and blend. Cook the pasta until al dente, drain it, return it to the pot, and mix in the pesto. Transfer to large warm bowls, taste for salt, pepper liberally, and top with the extra mint.

FOR INSTRUCTIONS ON COOKING EDAMAME, SEE PAGE 29.

Asparagus Pasta with Lemon and Shiso

This recipe couldn't be simpler, more refreshing, or more bulletproof. It's a quick, wonderful dinner in summer, when asparagus are peaking and overflowing in stores.... Try it with a big creamy California chardonnay. Any kind of pasta is fine here; I like penne and linguine.

■　■　■

SERVES 2

1 pound (450 gr) asparagus

pasta for 2, about ¹⁄₂ pound (225 gr)

20 shiso leaves

¹⁄₄ cup extra virgin olive oil

zest of 2 lemons

juice of 2 lemons

sea salt

fresh coarsely ground black pepper

¹⁄₄ cup freshly grated Parmesan cheese
(optional)

Set a large pot of salted water to boil. Snap off and discard the tough bottom ends of the asparagus. Slice off and reserve the tips. Boil the asparagus pieces (but not the tips) about 3 or 4 minutes, then add the tips, and cook for another minute. When done, remove them with a slotted spoon (reserving the water to boil the pasta) and put them in a bowl. Start cooking the pasta.

While the pasta is cooking, remove the tips and set aside (they will be served whole, on top of the pasta). Put the boiled asparagus in a blender, along with the shiso, olive oil, zest, lemon juice, salt, and pepper, and blend. If the blender has trouble moving, add a small amount of the pasta water (but you shouldn't need it).

When the pasta is al dente, scoop out a cup of the pasta water and set it aside. Drain the pasta and return it to the now-empty pot and add the blended asparagus. Turn the heat on high and stir everything together. Add some of the reserved pasta water, if needed, a little at a time, until the consistency feels just right. Liberally salt and pepper, and place portions in warmed serving bowls. Grate on some Parmesan, and top with the asparagus tips. Serve immediately, perhaps with a simple green salad.

Udon with Figs and Herbs

▌ This ultralight (and ultraquick) herb sauce goes perfectly with udon.

■ ■ ■

SERVES 2

1 fresh fig, or 1 large dried fig

1 cup parsley, chopped

10 shiso leaves, 1 reserved and sliced
  thinly

3 tablespoons extra virgin olive oil

juice of 1 lime (or lemon)

sea salt

fresh coarsely ground black pepper

udon for 2, about $\frac{1}{2}$ pound (225 gr)

zest of 1 lime (or lemon)

Set a pot of water to boil and set aside the udon. Remove the skin from the fresh fig, or, if using dried, reconstitute for 10 minutes in a small cup of boiled water and trim the ends. Put the fig and everything else but the zest into the blender, and blend. Cook the udon until al dente. Drain it, return it to the pot, add the sauce, and mix well. Transfer to large, warm bowls, taste for salt, and top with the reserved shiso and the zest.

Most noodle restaurants in Japan offer two choices: udon (thick wheat-flour noodles) and soba (thinner buckwheat noodles). Soba tastes better in a simple dashi broth. And because udon seems to stand up to assertive sauces better, I have used it exclusively here.

Shiitake Ginger Pasta Salad with Radicchio

This dish may look complicated, but it's not—it can be assembled in well under 30 minutes. Great with crusty bread, a salad, perhaps a simple piece of grilled fish; it's also a nice dish to bring to a potluck. Try it with a medium-bodied red like a grenache or even a merlot.

■　■　■

SERVES 4 HUNGRY PEOPLE

3 tablespoons olive oil

2 tablespoons butter

3 cups fresh white mushrooms, roughly
    chopped

1 cup fresh large shiitake mushrooms,
    roughly chopped

sea salt

fresh coarsely ground black pepper

3 tablespoons garlic, minced

3 tablespoons fresh ginger, minced

1 cup edamame, cooked and shelled

4 cups shredded radicchio

1/2 pound (225 gr) farfalle (bow-tie pasta)

1 heaping tablespoon Dijon mustard

splash of soy sauce

2 tablespoons red wine vinegar

Parmesan cheese (optional)

In a large wok or other pot, heat the oil and 1 tablespoon of the butter and sauté all the mushrooms, liberally salting and peppering them as they cook, until golden brown. In a small sauté pan, heat up the remaining tablespoon of the butter, sauté the garlic and ginger in it for 2 minutes, and add to the mushroom mixture. Add the edamame and radicchio and cook for another minute or two.

Set a large pot of water to boil for the farfalle. Cook the pasta until al dente, then drain it and stir it into the mushroom mixture. Toss the mixture and remove the wok from the heat. In a large bowl, whisk together the mustard, soy sauce, and vinegar, and dress the pasta with it. Adjust the salt, shave on some Parmesan, and serve in warm bowls.

FOR INSTRUCTIONS ON COOKING EDAMAME, SEE PAGE 29.

Mint-Cilantro Udon with Fresh Ginger and Meyer Lemon

This dish is so light that it almost floats! An excellent way to end a meal, or as a simple lunch. Use regular lemon if you can't find the more floral (and more interesting) Meyer variety. Total prep time is about 5 minutes.

■   ■   ■

SERVES 2

1 tablespoon extra virgin olive oil

1 tablespoon shallots, chopped

3 heaping tablespoons plain yogurt

1 cup fresh mint leaves, chopped

1 cup fresh cilantro leaves, chopped

1 tablespoon fresh ginger, diced

zest of 1 Meyer lemon, minced, 1 pinch reserved

juice of 1 Meyer lemon

sea salt

udon for 2, about ½ pound (225 gr)

Set a pot of water to boil for the udon. Heat the oil in a small skillet, sauté the shallots in it for a few minutes, and transfer them to a blender. Add everything else to the blender (except the udon, of course), and blend. Cook the udon until al dente, drain, return to the pot, and gently mix in the sauce from the blender. Taste for salt, transfer to warm plates, and sprinkle on the reserved zest.

Asian Pesto Udon

A satisfying and easy sauce that can be made in less time than it takes to boil the water. It's equally good hot or cold. Hot version: heat the sauce, serve over hot udon. Cold version: make the sauce, chill it, plunge the just-cooked noodles into ice water, and mix. Either way, it's nice with a chilled glass of dry riesling or semillon blend.

■ ■ ■

SERVES 2

½ cup smoked (or roasted) almonds

3 tablespoons fresh ginger, diced

1 tablespoon walnut (or other light) oil

½ cup coconut milk

1 tablespoon brown rice vinegar (or other vinegar)

2 tablespoons soy sauce

udon for 2, about ½ pound (225 gr)

1 cup cilantro, chopped (or to taste)

Set a pot of water to boil for the udon. Combine everything except the cilantro in a blender and blend. When the boils, add the udon and cook until al dente, and then drain. Transfer the sauce from the blender to the pot, add the udon, and mix. Taste for salt, top with the cilantro, and serve in warm bowls.

Meat

Using ginger, umeboshi, and soy sauce in innovative ways on meats yields delightful surprises for those who haven't yet experienced this pleasure. The dishes that follow are my Japanese-ish interpretations of some standards, with my usual twists of citrus and other fruit, herbs, and vinegars. I also adopt Japanese serving methods—all meat is sliced and prepared in the kitchen, to be served at the table and eaten with nothing but chopsticks. Using a knife at the table has somehow become vaguely unsettling to me; I've come to feel that all work should be done before one settles down to the very serious business of eating!

A word on shopping for meats: I think we have finally realized that local, grass-fed cows that live in decent, natural conditions actually taste better, and are probably a whole lot better for us. This meat costs a bit more, but the health and taste benefits seem well worth it. Try to use organic meats whenever you can.

Pan-Fried Rib-Eye Steaks with Ginger and Shallots

The ginger-shallot combination, along with the deglazed soy sauce, gives this a
rustic Japanesey flavor. Break out the big shiraz or old-vine zinfandel for this.

■ ■ ■

SERVES 2

2 tablespoons extra virgin olive oil

2 tablespoons very fresh ginger, minced

4 tablespoons shallots, minced

2 rib-eye steaks, cut about 1 inch (2.5 cm)
thick

2 tablespoons light soy sauce

In a heavy skillet, heat up 1 tablespoon of the olive oil and add the ginger and shallots. Sauté for a few minutes, until soft and well mixed. Transfer to a small bowl. In the same pan, heat up the other tablespoon of oil over very high heat and sear both sides of the steaks, leaving the inside pink or even a little raw. Transfer to a cutting board. Put the ginger and shallots back into the pan and add the soy sauce, mixing well. Cut into bite-sized pieces, transfer to warm plates, and pour the mixture over the slices. Have plenty of rice, potatoes, or bread around to go with it.

Spicy Pot Roast with Orange and Soy

Chinese cuisine has long combined orange, soy sauce, and beef to marvelous effect. This version follows that basic logic, applying it to pot roast. Good with a big bold petite syrah.

■ ■ ■

SERVES 4, AT LEAST

1 small pot roast or London broil, about 2 pounds (900 gr)

2 tablespoons extra virgin olive oil, plus additional for coating the pan

sea salt

coarsely ground fresh black pepper

½ teaspoon chipotle powder (or red pepper flakes)

juice of 2 oranges

zest of 2 oranges, minced finely

4 tablespoons soy sauce

a few orange segments (optional)

Preheat the oven to 375°F (190°C). Rinse the roast, pat it dry, rub it with 1 tablespoon of the olive oil, and salt and pepper it liberally. Heat the remaining tablespoon of oil in a heavy skillet large enough to accommodate the roast, and sear all sides over high heat until well browned.

Place the roast in a foil-lined oven pan coated lightly with olive oil, and sprinkle on the chipotle powder. Roast for about 30 minutes and check for desired doneness (the meat should be very tender). Remove it and let it rest. Put the pan drippings into a saucepan along with the orange juice, the zest, and the soy sauce, and simmer over medium heat for about 10 minutes, until the volume is reduced by half. Cool slightly, then slice the beef into bite-sized pieces, place on a large plate or platter, and pour on the reduced liquid. You may also want to cut up some additional orange segments and throw them in. The roast should already be salty enough, but check to make sure. Serve very hot, with potatoes or rice.

Baked Tonkatsu

Tonkatsu (pork cutlet) restaurants are ubiquitous in Japan and have an extremely loyal following. The traditional dish is breaded and deep-fried and served with a sweet sauce, but I much prefer this lower-fat and savory version. Any dry white or red seems to go well with this dish.

■ ■ ■

SERVES 3

3 meaty boneless pork chops or loins, about 1 pound (450 gr) total

sea salt

fresh coarsely ground black pepper

1 fresh jalapeño, seeds and veins removed, diced, or dried red pepper flakes or cayenne

3 tablespoons sweet pepper (orange, yellow, and red combo is nice), finely diced

3 tablespoons red onion, finely diced

zest of 1 orange, minced

½ cup seasoned breadcrumbs

You can easily make your own breadcrumbs by lightly toasting a piece of stale bread and then whirring it in a blender or spice grinder with dried oregano, thyme, and anything else you like.

Preheat oven to 400°F (200°C). Rinse the pork chops in cold water and dry with paper towels. Salt and pepper them, and place them in a foil-lined baking tray. Bake for about 5 minutes, remove from the oven and place on a cutting board. Drain and discard any juices that have accumulated in the pan (the meat should be rather dry for the next step).

Sprinkle on the jalapeño, then spoon on the sweet pepper and the red onion. Sprinkle on the orange zest. Finally, add the breadcrumbs, pressing them into the chops so that they stick. Return the chops to the oven and bake another 15 minutes or so, until nicely browned on top. Remove to a cutting board, cut into bite-sized strips, and serve on warm plates. Great with rice or baked potatoes.

Broiled Pork Loins with Dates, Umeboshi, and Walnuts

I never tire of this dish. The sweet stickiness of the dates, the crunch of the walnuts, and the piquancy of the umeboshi make for a delightful union with braised pork. A fruity merlot or cabernet rounds out the combination. Have plenty of rice around, and you have the main components of a fine meal.

■ ■ ■

SERVES 4

1 tablespoon butter	$^1\!/_2$ cup fresh carrot juice
5 tablespoons extra virgin olive oil	10 dried dates
1 medium-large red onion, diced	10 large umeboshi, pitted
1 teaspoon fresh rosemary, minced	4 pork loins, about 1 pound (450 gr) total
sea salt	$^1\!/_4$ cup walnuts
freshly ground black pepper	

Heat the butter and 3 tablespoons of the oil in a heavy skillet, add the onion, rosemary, salt, and pepper, and sauté for about 5 minutes. Transfer to a blender and add 1 tablespoon of the olive oil, the carrot juice, 5 of the dates, and 5 of the umeboshi, and blend.

In the same skillet, heat the remaining tablespoon of olive oil, lightly salt and pepper the loins, and sear both sides until well browned. Add the contents of the blender to the pan, pouring it around the meat. Bring to a boil, cover, turn down the heat to low, and cook for 30 minutes.

While it's braising, on a cutting board chop the 5 remaining dates, the 5 remaining umeboshi, and the walnuts, mixing them all together well. Transfer the meat to a cutting board, chop it up however you like, and serve on large hot plates, pouring any remaining pan juices over the meat. Top with the date-umeboshi-walnut mixture.

Lamb Shoulder with Apricot Mint and Ginger Sauce

Mint has always gone well with lamb, but this version adds ginger. The apricot jam helps to caramelize the meat, which gets extremely tender from the braising. Syrah gets the nod as an accompaniment.

■　■　■

SERVES 3 TO 4

4 tablespoons extra virgin olive oil

sea salt

fresh coarsely ground black pepper

3 lamb shoulder chops, about 1 1/2 pounds
    (650–700 gr) total

1 medium onion, chopped

3 tablespoons fresh ginger, minced

1 heaping tablespoon apricot jam

1 1/2 cups fresh mint, chopped

3 tablespoons apple juice (or orange juice)

Heat 2 tablespoons of the olive oil in a heavy skillet. Salt and pepper the lamb and brown both sides over high heat. While that's cooking, heat up the other 2 tablespoons of olive oil in a smaller skillet and sauté the onion and ginger with some salt and pepper. When the onion mixture softens, put it in a blender, together with the jam, all but a few tablespoons of the mint, and the apple juice, and blend. Pour this mixture over the lamb, stir a bit, cover, turn down the heat, and cook another 30 minutes or so, until the meat is very tender. Watch it carefully—the sugars will caramelize and burn if the heat is too high or if the liquid disappears. If it needs more liquid, add some more apple juice. Transfer to warm serving plates, taste for salt, spoon on any remaining sauce, and top with the reserved mint. Serve very hot, with rice or potatoes.

Grilled Marmalade "Bacon" with Meyer Lemon and Ginger

This delightful and easy dish takes about 10 minutes to prepare and cook. The idea is to slice the lean pork very thinly, so that it doesn't require much cooking time at all, which is necessary because the sugars in the marmalade will brown very quickly under a hot broiler. Good with rice, some pickles, and perhaps a salad or other vegetable side dish. Or great with poached eggs and a mimosa on a Sunday morning.

■ ■ ■

SERVES 2

½ pound (225 gr) very lean pork (sukiyaki-cut), sliced thinly

1 tablespoon extra virgin olive oil

1 tablespoon orange marmalade

zest of 1 Meyer lemon

juice of ½ Meyer lemon

coarse salt

fresh coarsely ground black pepper

Place the pork slices on a broiling rack and spoon (or, even better, spray) the olive oil over them to coat. Mix the marmalade, zest, and juice in a cup, and spoon the mixture on. Dust with salt and pepper, and broil over high heat for a few minutes on both sides, until nicely browned. Transfer to a warm plate. Taste for salt.

Poultry

Nothing comforts like a house permeated with the smell of chicken baking in the oven. Chicken aroma for the soul.

The explosion of humanely farmed organic chickens means both we and the birds are a lot luckier than we used to be; setting the politics of chicken aside, they just *taste* so much better than their industrially produced brothers. How could they not?

None of the techniques presented here are especially Japanese. Yakitori—skewered chicken, grilled and seasoned—is the method of choice in Japan. Simmered and deep-fried dishes are both popular, but chicken is rarely baked. It's the ingredients used that make these dishes identifiably Japanese, with a contemporary and playful spin.

Rice Vinegar Chicken Breasts

This classic recipe is tweaked with a Japanese touch: rice vinegar and soy sauce. The piquancy of the reduced vinegar seems to bring out the best and most natural flavor of chicken. The intense vinegar flavor makes it a tough wine pair, but a fruity viognier often hits the spot.

■ ■ ■

SERVES 2

4 tablespoons light soy sauce

1 tablespoon maple syrup

2 boneless chicken breasts, skins on,
    about 1 pound (450 gr)

fresh coarsely ground black pepper

3 tablespoons shallots, minced

1 tablespoon fresh thyme leaves, minced

2 tablespoons olive oil

1/2 cup rice vinegar

1 tablespoon unsalted butter (optional)

Turn the broiler on high. Combine 3 tablespoons of the soy sauce and the maple syrup in a bowl and mix. Marinate the breasts in it for a few minutes and pepper them. Broil them, skin side up, in the broiler under maximum heat until they turn deeply golden brown. Turn and broil the other side until nicely browned. Both sides should be crisp and well done, and the middle should be barely cooked through and very juicy.

While they're broiling, sauté the shallots with the thyme in the warmed olive oil for 2 or 3 minutes. If you can collect any of the juices from the breasts that accumulate in the bottom of the broiler pan, pour those into the skillet. Add the vinegar and the remaining tablespoon of soy sauce, raise the heat, and quickly bring to a boil. Simmer about 5 minutes, until the liquid is reduced by about half—it will be sharp and powerful on the tongue. Adding the butter at this stage will give the sauce a silky, rich texture.

On a cutting board, cut the breasts into bite-sized strips, and arrange them neatly on a warm plate. Spoon the liquid over, taste for salt, and give them a final flick of pepper.

Soy-Tarragon Chicken with Green Onion and Shallots

This dish is deeply savory and satisfying. It will disappear quickly, so you may want to consider doubling the recipe! You'll need a full bottle of unoaked chardonnay nearby.

■ ■ ■

SERVES 3 OR 4

4 tablespoons extra virgin olive oil

½ cup shallots, minced

½ cup chopped green onion tops

2 tablespoons light soy sauce

½ cup chopped tarragon

plenty of coarsely ground black pepper

1½ pounds (650–700 gr) boneless chicken thighs, most fat removed

sea salt

Preheat the oven to 400°F (200°C). Heat 1 tablespoon of the olive oil in a small nonstick skillet and sauté the shallots and green onion tops for a few minutes. Transfer them to a blender, add another tablespoon of the oil, the soy sauce, tarragon, and black pepper, and blend. If you need a little extra liquid to allow the blender to do its work, add a little more soy sauce or leftover stock.

Rinse and dry the chicken with paper towels. Cut away most of the excess fat/skin. Cut the thighs into medium-large pieces.

In a large pan or wok, heat the remaining 2 tablespoons of olive oil on maximum heat, add the chicken pieces, and season liberally with salt and pepper. Shake the pan frequently to keep them from sticking, and cook for about 5 minutes per side, until the chicken begins to brown. While it's cooking, line an oven pan with aluminum foil (to make cleanup easy), and coat the foil lightly with olive oil. When the chicken has browned, transfer it to the oven pan and add the contents of the blender. Mix thoroughly, making sure all the pieces are well coated. Pepper them a little more, and bake about 35 minutes, until very well done.

Soy-Brined Roasted Turkey with Ruby Grapefruit and Fennel Gravy

It's a shame that most people cook turkey only on Thanksgiving and Christmas; this festive version could be a monthly event! I like to brine (soak in water or stock flavored with sugar and salt) the bird overnight, which keeps the meat extremely moist. This is not necessary, but it does give a more flavorful and moist turkey. The roasting requires some care, but the results are well worth it. An iced bottle or two of good champagne to go with this turkey will ensure a memorable evening.

■ ■ ■

SERVES MANY

THE BRINE:

3 cups soy sauce

$\frac{1}{2}$ cup brown sugar

1 young turkey, about 12 pounds (5 $\frac{1}{2}$ kg)

water or stock to cover the bird

Pour the soy sauce into a large bucket or other vessel large enough to hold the turkey, add the sugar, and mix. Add the turkey and enough water or stock to cover. Add some ice if you're cooking this in summer, or squeeze it into the refrigerator. Brine overnight, or for at least several hours.

THE DISH:

1 tablespoon olive oil

2 tablespoons fresh thyme leaves, minced

1 ruby grapefruit, cut into eighths (the peel stays on)

fresh coarsely ground black pepper

1 large fennel bulb, roughly chopped

1 large red onion, roughly chopped

sea salt

Preheat the oven to 425°F (220°C). Rinse the bird, dry it thoroughly with paper towels, and rub the olive oil all over it, including inside the cavity. Sprinkle the thyme inside the cavity, then stuff the cut-up grapefruit into the cavity, and place the bird in a foil-lined baking pan outfitted with a rack to allow the fat to drip. Pepper the whole thing liberally and make a little aluminum foil tent to avoid burning the skin. Cook the turkey about 45 minutes, take it out, discard the tent, and with a sharp knife lightly slice the place where the leg meets the body, to ensure thorough cooking there. Turn it over, reduce the heat to 300°F (150°C), and roast for 1 hour. Add the fennel and onion to the bottom of the pan, amid the juices, turn the heat back up to 400°F (200°C), and roast another 15 minutes. Take it out and turn it again and continue to roast another 15 to 30 minutes. The bird should be deeply browned by now—if not, keep cooking till it is. Total cooking time should be about 2 1/2 hours.

When done, remove it from the oven and let it rest for a while. Collect the fennel, onions, and the juices, and blend them in a blender to make a gravy. Remove the grapefruit wedges, and set aside.

To carve, cut off the legs first, then the wings. The meat should basically just fall off the bones (if it doesn't, it needs to be cooked a little more). Then slice the breast down the middle, pulling the meat off with the knife. Cut into bite-sized pieces. Transfer all the meat to a warm platter, squeeze the roasted grapefruit wedges over the meat, mix in the gravy, liberally salt and pepper, and serve hot.

Baked Onion Chicken Thighs with Umeboshi and Shiso

Umeboshi (Japanese pickled plums) and shiso is a natural and traditional combination in Japan (especially in sushi), but the sautéed onions blended into the
mixture give it a new and satisfying depth that permeates the chicken. Wonderful with hot rice, miso soup, and a small flask of chilled sake.

■ ■ ■

SERVES 2 OR 3

6 tablespoons extra virgin olive oil, plus
    additional for the baking dish
1 large onion, minced
sea salt
fresh coarsely ground black pepper
10 umeboshi, pitted

20 shiso leaves, chopped, 1 tablespoon
    reserved
splash of sake
1 pound (450 gr) boneless, skinless
    chicken thighs

Preheat the oven to 400°F (200°C). In a heavy skillet over high heat,
heat 3 tablespoons of the olive oil, add the onion, and liberally salt and
pepper. Sauté until soft, about 5 minutes. Place the onion in the blender
and add the umeboshi, shiso, and 1 tablespoon of the olive oil, and blend
(also add as much sake as the blender needs to do its work). Reserve
about 3 tablespoons of this mixture in a small bowl. In the same skillet,
heat up the 2 remaining tablespoons of oil over maximum heat and fry
the chicken until brown spots begin to appear. Transfer the chicken and
the blended onion mixture to a large bowl and mix. Apply or spray
some olive oil to a baking dish, transfer the chicken to it, and bake until
golden, about 30 minutes. Remove the chicken, mix the reserved sauce
through it, and return it to the oven for another few minutes before
serving. Serve on a warm plate, topped off with the chopped shiso.

Persimmon Balsamic Chicken

I make this dish a lot when the kaki (persimmons) are in season. Kaki seem custom-made for vinegar and chicken. A bottle of California zinfandel will be in order.

■ ■ ■

SERVES 4

1 large persimmon, peeled, seeded, and
    roughly chopped
¼ cup balsamic vinegar
1 tablespoon extra virgin olive oil, plus
    additional for rubbing the chicken
4 tablespoons fresh tarragon, minced,
    1 tablespoon reserved

1 tablespoon soy sauce
sea salt
fresh coarsely ground black pepper
4 boneless chicken breasts, skins on,
    2 pounds (900 gr)

You can discard the skin if you want to avoid the extra fat/calories. If you do, you may want to regrill/rebroil the meat just under the skin for a minute or two.

Preheat the broiler or light the barbecue. Into the blender put the persimmon, vinegar, 1 tablespoon of the olive oil, 2 tablespoons of the tarragon, soy sauce, and pepper, and blend. Transfer the mixture to a small saucepan and bring to a rapid boil, then turn the heat way down to low. Continue to simmer until the volume is reduced by about half (about 15 minutes).

Meanwhile, pound the chicken breasts to flatten and even them, and rub them with some olive oil. Salt and pepper liberally, and broil or grill, skin side toward the heat, about 3 or 4 minutes, until nicely browned. Turn them over and spoon on some of the sauce. Broil or grill for another few minutes, until bubbly and browned. Transfer to a warm dish, spoon on some extra sauce. Taste for salt and sprinkle on the 2 remaining tablespoons of tarragon.

Potatoes and Rice

Starches and carbohydrates go in and out of vogue, but I remain a diehard fan. I like potatoes or rice as a main dish, or as a complement to a meal. Rice is traditionally eaten last in Japanese restaurants, on the theory that it's not good to fill up on it until you've really tasted everything else. This custom makes sense for kaiseki-style dining (seasonal cuisine brought out in up to 20 small courses), but for home cooking, I often like to have my starch right in front of me at all times!

Unplain Rice

This is my standard rice; I like to use it as most people would use regular cooked white rice.

Rinse any quantity of rice that you like (about 2 cups is my normal amount), and put it in a nonstick pot with a tight-fitting lid. Level out the rice with your hand. Next, barely touch the tip of your index finger to the level of the rice. Add your liquid until the liquid level hits just below the first joint of your finger. In other words, the distance between rice level and liquid is the distance from your fingertip to the first joint, or a little less than an inch. Be sure the rice is level when you "measure." This method works, regardless of how much rice you are making or the size of the vessel.

But instead of using just water as your liquid, use a ratio of one-third carrot juice to two-thirds water. (Do not use vegetable juice—it's not nearly as good.) Then add 1 heaping tablespoon Dijon mustard, and 5 or

6 bay leaves, and mix it all together with a wooden spoon. Bring it to a boil, cover tightly, turn down the heat to very low, and cook for about 20 minutes for japonica rice, slightly less for basmati or Thai rice. Your rice will take on a rich orange-salmon color, give off subtly sweet hints of laurel, and will have slightly more body than regular rice, thanks to the mustard. When the rice is done, discard the bay leaves first, mix well, and add salt if you wish. Use exactly as you would normal white rice.

Curried Apple Pilaf

This rice fills the house with its aromatic intensity as it cooks. Fine as a meal on its own, or as a special accompaniment to an entrée.

■ ■ ■

SERVES 3 OR 4

2 tablespoons olive oil

1 medium onion, diced

sea salt

fresh coarsely ground black pepper

1 tablespoon very fresh garlic, minced
    (about 3 or 4 cloves)

2 tablespoons fresh ginger, minced

1/2 teaspoon curry powder

1 cup rice, rinsed

1/2 teaspoon cinnamon

1 Fuji (or other) apple, peeled, cored, diced

1 cup hot water

1 cup fresh carrot juice

2 tablespoons slivered (or diced) almonds

3 tablespoons fresh cilantro, chopped

Heat the oil over high heat in a large pot, add the onion, liberally salt and pepper, and cook for about 5 minutes, shaking the pan often to keep it from burning. Add the garlic, ginger, and curry powder, and cook for another minute or so. Stir in the rice, the cinnamon, and half of the apple, and continue to cook for another minute. Add the water and carrot juice, and bring to a boil. Stir, cover, reduce the heat to very low, and cook until the pilaf is done, about 15 minutes. In the meantime, toast the almonds, either in a dry skillet or a toaster oven. Transfer the pilaf to a bowl, add the remaining half of the apple, and taste for salt (it may need quite a bit). Sprinkle on the cilantro, then the almonds, and serve hot.

Mashed Ginger Sweet Potatoes

The sweetness of the potatoes melds beautifully with the ginger and yogurt to produce these fluffy creations that everyone seems to love. Serve them with chicken or fish.

■ ■ ■

MAKES 6 OR 7 LARGE SERVINGS

3 medium-large sweet potatoes, or yams	4 tablespoons fresh ginger, minced
2 tablespoons extra virgin olive oil	1 egg
sea salt	1 tablespoon soy sauce
fresh coarsely ground black pepper	4 tablespoons plain yogurt
1 tablespoon butter	2 tablespoons milk
½ cup shallots, minced	

Preheat the oven to 375°F (190°C). Rub the potatoes with 1 tablespoon of the olive oil, liberally salt and pepper them, and roast about 40 minutes, or until tender. Meanwhile, in a small pan, heat the butter and the remaining tablespoon of oil, add the shallots and ginger, salt and pepper, and sauté for about 5 minutes, until soft. Transfer to a blender, add the egg and soy sauce, and blend.

Remove the potatoes when done, let them cool a bit, and peel off the skins. Transfer to a large mixing bowl, add the yogurt and milk, and mix well, using a sturdy wooden spoon and plenty of elbow grease. Add the egg-ginger mixture from the blender, and again mix thoroughly. Salt and pepper to taste.

Boozy Japanese Potatoes

The burst of sake on the tongue that these potatoes bring out is a pleasant surprise, and a perfect union with the soy sauce. These potatoes are a natural with meat or fish, and especially with dishes that are flavored with Asian ingredients like ginger.

■ ■ ■

SERVES 3 OR 4

3 medium potatoes (Yukon Golds are great here)

3 tablespoons extra virgin olive oil

1 1/2 cups sake

2 tablespoons soy sauce

1 tablespoon butter

Set a large pot of water to boil. Peel the potatoes and cut them into eighths. Add them to the boiling water and cook for about 10 minutes. Don't overboil; they should retain their shape, but still be somewhat tender. They should still have a bite to them, since they will be cooked in sake later. When tender but firm, drain them in a colander.

Heat the oil over high heat in a large nonstick skillet and add the potato pieces. Move the pan around so that all are coated nicely with the oil. Cook on high heat for about 5 minutes, shaking the pan occasionally and browning them slightly. Add the sake (it will sizzle noisily), and continue to cook on high heat for another 5 minutes or so, shaking the pan often, until the sake almost disappears. Add the soy sauce and shake again, coating the potatoes with a nice thick brown sauce, and turn the heat down to low. Taste one—if it needs more soy sauce, add it. Add the butter, stir, and cook another 5 minutes; they should be brown and crispy on the outside. Serve immediately on warm plates.

Rosemary Shiso Potato Crisps

These potatoes have some of the crispiness of a potato chip, and the savory depth of a potato roasted with herbs; the best of both worlds, really. They go well with steak or any grilled meat.

■ ■ ■

SERVES 3, 4, OR MORE

3 large russet potatoes, skins on, washed and sliced into ¼- or ½-inch (1-cm) rounds, depending on preference

olive oil for rubbing on the potatoes

sea salt

freshly ground pepper

4 tablespoons fresh rosemary, minced

20 shiso leaves, minced, plus 5 additional leaves, minced

Preheat the oven to 425°F (220°C). On a large cutting board, lay the potato slices out individually. Rub or spray olive oil over each, salt and pepper them, and sprinkle on half the rosemary and half the shiso. Move them to a foil-lined baking pan outfitted with a broiling rack, and arrange them in one layer, avoiding crowding (don't overlap, or they won't cook evenly; do it in two rounds if you have to). Bake for about 15 to 20 minutes, until brown spots begin to appear and the edges are crisp. Remove from the oven, turn them over one by one, and spray or spoon on more olive oil, salt and pepper liberally, and add the second half of the rosemary and shiso. Turn up the oven to 500°F (260°C) and bake for another 5 minutes or so, until they look crispy. Serve hot, giving them a final sprinkle of shiso, and taste for salt.

Vegetable Side Dishes

Native Japanese vegetables are delightful beyond measure, especially the sea vegetables and the seasonal wild vegetables. Unfortunately, they are hard to find outside Japan, and thus have not been included here. Instead, I've focused on easy-to-find vegetables and added Japanese touches to them.

If you're lucky enough to have a local farmers' market, you really should take advantage of it. Farmers' markets often beat the big supermarkets on price, and the food will be locally grown. It will also have been raised with little or no pesticides, and it will taste like the essence of real food.

Hot Vegetable Summer Salad with Miso Vinaigrette

The shiso and miso give these vegetables a "fresh" spin that people seem to love.

■ ■ ■

SERVES 3 OR 4

2 ears very fresh corn, shucked

2 tablespoons extra virgin olive oil

1 small to medium zucchini, roughly
    chopped

1 small bag (about ¼ pound/110 gr)
    fresh green beans, ends trimmed,
    cut in 1-inch (2.5-cm) pieces

sea salt

fresh coarsely ground black pepper

2 tablespoons walnut oil

2 tablespoons brown rice (or other) vinegar

1 tablespoon miso

1 teaspoon apricot jam

10 shiso leaves, minced

1 tablespoon chives, minced

Cut the kernels from the cob into a bowl. Warm the olive oil in a large frying pan, add the corn, zucchini, and green beans. Salt and pepper them, and cook over medium heat for about 5 minutes. Meanwhile, combine the walnut oil, vinegar, miso, and apricot jam in a cup and mix, to make a vinaigrette. Add this to the pan, mixing gently but thoroughly. Add the shiso and mix again. Taste for salt, and serve on warm plates. Top with chives.

Cherried Carrots with Ginger

The orange-red color of this simple and somewhat sweet dish adds festivity to any meal.

■ ■ ■

SERVES 3, 4, OR MORE

2 tablespoons extra virgin olive oil

2 tablespoons fresh ginger, minced

1 pound (450 gr) carrots, peeled and
    sliced on the diagonal

sea salt

fresh coarsely ground black pepper

20 Bing cherries, pitted and chopped

¼ cup fresh carrot juice

2 tablespoons light soy sauce

1 tablespoon Italian parsley, chopped

Baby carrots, used whole, work well in this dish.

Heat 1 tablespoon of the olive oil over high heat in a large saucepan, add the ginger and carrots, season them generously with salt and pepper, and cook over high heat for about 5 minutes, stirring occasionally. Meanwhile, put half the cherries in a blender with the carrot juice, the soy sauce, and the remaining tablespoon of olive oil, and blend. Add this to the carrots, stir, and turn down the heat to medium. Cook for about 10 more minutes, until the liquid disappears. Taste for salt, and mix in the remaining cherries. Transfer to a warm bowl, adjust the salt, and top with the parsley.

Orange Tarragon Cauliflower Simmered in Sake

The combination of sake, orange, and cauliflower may not be well known, but it's fabulous, and the tarragon adds a whole new layer of complexity. If you can find purple cauliflower, so much the better—it's one of the few purple foods that keeps its color after cooking. The dish becomes even more fragrant if you can find yuzu, a Japanese citrus, to replace the orange.

■　■　■

SERVES 3 OR 4

1 medium head cauliflower

2 tablespoons olive oil

1 tablespoon garlic, minced

sea salt

freshly ground pepper

juice of 1 orange (or yuzu)

½ cup sake

1 tablespoon light soy sauce

zest of 1 orange (or yuzu), minced

4 tablespoons fresh tarragon, chopped,
    a little reserved

Cut the cauliflower in half, then cut away the tough stem. Chop the florets and softer parts of the stem quite finely; the pieces should be the size and consistency of granola. In a large skillet, heat the oil on high, add the cauliflower and garlic, and season generously with salt and pepper. Cook over high heat for 5 minutes, stirring often. Squeeze the orange juice into the pan (which will cause it to sizzle). Add the sake and soy sauce, quickly bring to a boil, stir, reduce the heat, and cook until the liquid disappears. Add the zest and most of the tarragon, mix well, and continue to cook for a few more minutes, until the cauliflower begins to brown a bit. Taste for salt. Top with the remaining tarragon, and serve on warm plates or bowls.

Roasted Butternut Squash with Tarragon and Rice Vinegar

The anise-like flavors of the tarragon marry well with the rich flesh of the squash. A nice accompaniment to any meat dish.

■ ■ ■

SERVES 4 OR 5, AT LEAST

1 medium butternut squash, about 2 pounds (900 gr)	sea salt
	coarsely ground black pepper
3 tablespoons extra virgin olive oil	1 tablespoon light soy sauce
2 tablespoon shallots, minced	3 tablespoons rice vinegar
5 tablespoons fresh tarragon, chopped	juice of 1 clementine

A mandarin orange or tangerine can be substituted for the clementine.

Preheat the oven to 425°F (220°C). Remove the seeds and fibers of the squash, slice off the tough skin, and cut it into bite-sized pieces of various shapes. Put them in a large ceramic oven-safe bowl (Japanese *donabe* are perfect for this), add the olive oil, shallots, and tarragon, and mix thoroughly. Liberally salt and pepper, and mix in the soy sauce. Bake for about 35 minutes, or until tender. Remove, gently mix in the vinegar and the juice, and taste for salt.

Greens and Oranges

This is a marvelously simple and delicious way to eat lots of greens.

■ ■ ■

SERVES 2 OR 3

2 bunches of greens (any non-lettuce
    greens, like spinach, kale, or collard
    greens, will do)
several tablespoons extra virgin olive oil
1 or 2 tablespoons brown rice vinegar (or
    other vinegar), to taste
sea salt

fresh coarsely ground black pepper
juice of 1/4 orange (or other orange citrus)
several orange sections, all membranes
    removed
zest of 1 orange (or other orange citrus),
    minced

Set a pot of water to boil. Rinse and trim the greens of imperfections and boil them briefly for several minutes. Drain and rinse with cold water. When slightly cooled, squeeze out as much excess water as possible (you can save this mineral-laden water if you wish, for making rice or soup stock). Place the squeezed greens on a cutting board and roughly chop. Put them in a bowl and add the olive oil, vinegar, and salt and pepper. Mix and adjust the taste. Squeeze the orange juice over the greens, add a few orange sections, and sprinkle the zest over. Serve at room temperature.

ACKNOWLEDGMENTS

Special thanks go to the team who made this happen: Elizabeth Floyd, my tireless and extraordinary editor; Kazuhiko Miki, the man responsible for the luscious design of the book; and Fumihiko Watanabe, the photographer who lent his acute sensibility and unerring eye to the project. Thanks too to Haruko and Barry Lancet, Shigeyoshi Suzuki, and Hideko and Akio Terakura for trusting us with their exquisite pottery, and to Stephen Shaw, who believed in the book from the very beginning. In the best of mom traditions, my mother, Kathy Joe Gower, showers me with love and support no matter what I'm working on. Thanks Joe! Bill "the saint" Campbell in Tokyo graciously provided the best kitchen, wine, and friendship one could ask for, when I needed them most.

Glass maestro Reiko Sasaki was invaluable as my assistant during the photography. Valerie Koehn has been a fount of support, in every way, and I'm indebted to her generosity of spirit. The Saint Helena, California home of Kathy and Caleb Shuey was the site of lots of culinary experimentation, and to them I'm grateful. A tip of the beer glass to the Kamakura frisbee crew for all the gastronomic (and other) fun we've had over the years. To Debbie Gross and Charles Haynes and their magical house and kitchen on Walter Street in San Francisco, where many of these recipes were tested, I have a mountain of gratitude. And finally to Karen Riley, for whom most of these recipes (and many others) were lovingly made. What a lineup of people to have in your corner.

NOTES AND DEFINITIONS

Chipotle: Dried, smoked jalapeño peppers. The powdered form is a delicious and very powerful spice. Also sold whole, in cans, typically in a tomato-based adobo sauce.

Dashi: Classic Japanese stock. Made from simmering a stick of konbu (kelp), and adding the shavings of some katsuobushi (dried bonito). Used heavily throughout Japanese cuisine.

Edamame: Soybeans, sold both in the pod and shelled, usually frozen. If using shelled beans, they typically come precooked; simply thaw them in the microwave or briefly soak them in hot water. If using edamame with pods, boil or steam them for about five minutes, drain, rinse with cold water, and shell into a bowl. They're fun to pop from the shells for snacks, and go great with beer.

Extra virgin olive oil: So many kinds! Best to experiment widely. I really like the bright green, extra fruity ones.

Ginger: Always use the freshest you can find. Asian grocery stores are likely to have fresher and cheaper ginger than big supermarkets. Baby ginger (shinshoga), as the name implies, is more tender and not as pungent; it's wonderful pickled. *See also* gari, page 109.

Herbs: The best source for fresh herbs is within easy reach: during the warm months, it's very easy to grow (even on a veranda) small pots of mint, basil, Italian parsley, thyme, rosemary, and oregano. If you have a small yard, so much the better. Nothing is more satisfying than to walk out, pinch off what you need for dinner, and start using it.

If you can't grow your own, fresh herbs are, thankfully, available in most supermarkets nowadays, though they can be pricey if youre a heavy user like I am. I buy those in winter.

Kabocha: Japanese pumpkin, with dark green skin and sweet yellow flesh. Can be used as any other squashes are used.

Kabosu: Japanese green citrus, about the size of a small lime. Good for both juice and zest.

Konbu: Dried kelp traditionally used with dried bonito flakes to make dashi (stock for soups and simmered dishes). One dried stick, typically about 6 inches (15 centimeters) long and weighing perhaps 1 ounce (30 grams), is the usual amount needed. Using a little less or a little more will vary the intensity of the flavor. Experiment with quantity; determine the level you yourself like best.

Meyer lemon: Believed to be a hybrid of the common Eureka lemon and mandarin orange. Significantly sweeter and more floral than regular lemons.

Miso: Salted and fermented soybean paste eaten daily by nearly everyone in Japan, usually in the form of a simple soup in the morning and evening. Experiment with as many varieties as you can find (yellow, red, etc.).

Nam pla: Widely used in Southeast Asia as a salty condiment, much like soy sauce is used in Japan. Made from fermented fish; can be an acquired taste!

Pepper: Never buy pre-ground pepper—it will ruin whatever it touches. Most people grind their pepper with a pepper mill. I much prefer to grind mine in a mortar or spice grinder (or coffee mill), and pour the roughly ground pepper into a small ceramic bowl that sits right next to my salt near the stove. That way I can just reach in and grab whatever amount I need. It's faster and more accurate than the mill, and only requires one hand.

It is aesthetically pleasing for some reason to use pepper that varies in its coarseness; some of the peppercorns will be barely crushed, while the pepper in other parts of the bowl will be finely ground. A pinch with your fingers will typically pick up both.

Persimmon: All recipes refer to Fuyu persimmons, which vaguely resemble an orange tomato, with a flat bottom. The pointed-end Hachiya persimmons are also delicious, but must be used when the fruit turns almost liquid; otherwise they will be very unpleasantly astringent.

Ponzu: Dipping sauce for cooked meats, fish, and vegetables. The classic version is made with dashi, soy sauce, and citrus juice, but it can also include vinegar, mirin, citrus zest, fruit, and chilis.

Rice: Japonica is sacrosanct in Japan, and is practically the only kind available here. There is no question that Japonica goes well with Japanese food, so I encourage its use for the recipes in this book, but for those lucky enough to have access to other kinds, the more experimentation the better. I don't use a rice cooker, but pretty much every Japanese person does.

Rice vinegar: I avoid the big-name makers and opt instead for the smaller, more interesting vinegars available in Japanese markets; they just have more character. Brown rice vinegar is always worth keeping around.

Sake: Fermented rice wine. For the recipes in this book, cheaper sake is fine, since we're only cooking with it. For drinking, I encourage you to try some of the finer premium sakes now widely available. Serve them chilled.

Salt: Use kosher salt or sea salt—the crystals are bigger, it feels better in your fingers, and it tastes more like a spice than regular iodized salt. I like to keep it in small bowls, one by the stove and one on the table.

Sesame oil: Comes in light, and dark (from toasted sesame, which has a nuttier, more intense flavor).

Shiitake: Japan's most popular mushroom, sold both fresh and dried.

Shiso: Also known as perilla, and, to the amusement of many Japanese, as beefsteak plant. Its flavor is unique —pungent and grassy, it contains strong flavors of spearmint, basil, and even cinnamon, especially when sliced into a chiffonade. Its buds are especially delicious, and pack an enormous amount of flavor.

Soba: Thin buckwheat noodles, very popular throughout Japan. I especially like the green cha-soba, soba made with green tea added.

Soy sauce (shoyu): I prefer the lighter soy sauce (usukuchi shoyu), both for color and taste reasons, though it tends to have a slightly higher salt content than darker versions. The light brown color means that it can be added without turning food dark, and the taste is more subtle than the overpowering darker forms like tamari. Experiment with the smaller, gourmet-type varieties available in Japanese markets.

Sudachi: Small Japanese limes, but with a decidedly perfumey hint. Imagine a small Meyer lime.

Tataki: Method of cooking in which meats and fish are seared over high heat, and the middle is left undercooked or raw.

Tofu: Soybean curd. The custard-like oborodofu, also sometimes called yosedofu, is the tofu of choice, but try the silken variety if you can't find it.

Togarashi: Red chili peppers, crushed, often blended with other ingredients. The blended variety is sometimes referred to as shichimi. Typically used sprinkled over udon, soba, tempura, yakitori, and nabe.

Udon: Wheat noodles, typically used in dashi-based broths.

Umeboshi: Pickled, salty plums, typically eaten at the end of a meal to aid digestion. They can be outrageously sour (and utterly delicious). Mind the pits.

Yuzu: The fruit produces little juice, and is mostly prized for its zest, which seems to combine the best of orange, lemon, lime, and tangerine. Used in soups, in custard dishes, and on grilled fish. Often mixed with soy sauce to make a dipping sauce known as ponzu. Makes a wonderful addition to salad dressings; adds elegance to everything it touches.

Zest: The colored peel of any citrus, typically minced. Should contain no white bitter pith. Special tools called zesters are extremely handy for this job. One of those, the Microplane zester, is especially good.

Gari

In my enthusiasm for gari—the pickled ginger served alongside sushi—I discovered that not only is the ginger delicious, the vinegar in which the ginger is pickled is, too. It takes on a spectacularly vibrant ginger-infused flavor, which I like to use in salad dressings, sauces, on fish . . . anyplace you'd use ordinary vinegar. Before I started experimenting with it, I'd never seen gari made with any vinegar other than rice vinegar, but it quickly became clear that you can make balsamic gari, raspberry gari, tarragon white wine gari, ad infinitum. They're all good, and all very different. The formula is the same for all: 1 part vinegar added to 1 part shaved fresh ginger, plus a little sweetener. Try this one:

1 cup very thinly sliced (shaved) fresh ginger
½ cup black raspberry vinegar
½ cup rice vinegar
3 tablespoons maple syrup

Set a small saucepan of water to boil. Peel the ginger and, with a mandoline, slice it very thinly until you have 1 cup of it (one large root will accomplish this). Blanch in the boiling water for about 2 minutes. Drain and transfer to a jar big enough to comfortably hold it. Pour the vinegars and maple syrup into the saucepan, stir, bring to a simmer, and pour into the jar. Let cool, and place in the refrigerator. Keeps forever (well, at least a month).

—*Caveat*: the high sugar content of balsamic makes it slightly different than other vinegars; you may want to use less sweetener when using it.—

INDEX

SELECTED POTTERY, GLASSWARE, AND CLOTH CREDITS

POTTERY

SHIRO TSUJIMURA
61 Slipware plate
78–79 Rectangular slipware platter
99 Shino-ware teabowl

KAI TSUJIMURA
86 Large Karatsu-style stoneware bowl
104 Shigaraki-ware plate
106 Large Karatsu-style stoneware bowl

JURGEN LEHL
11 Porcelain bowl
19 Large stoneware plate
31 Porcelain bowl
91 Porcelain bowl

MITSURU KOIZUMI
25 Lacquered rope-coil plates
89 Lacquered rope-coil bowl

BEN COHEN
58 Wood-fired Echizen-ware dish

REIKO COHEN
5 (TOP) Wood-fired Echizen-ware plates
65 Wood-fired Echizen-ware platter

ATSUO YAMAGISHI
2 (BACK) Red lacquer bowls
25, 89 Lacquer spoons
39 Red lacquer bowls
50–51 Large lacquer fork and spoon

JINENBO NAKAGAWA
94 Karatsu-ware dish

KIYOSHI HARA
Cover Large celadon plate

GLASSWARE

REIKO SASAKI
17 Streaked fused-glass plate
27 Blown-glass bowl
43 Small blown-glass bowl
55 Streaked fused-glass plate
66 Striped fused-glass plate

CLOTH

YOSHIKO JINZENJI
27 Bamboo-dyed silk shibori
100 Cotton dyed with indigo and persimmon tannin

NUNO CORPORATION
11 "Tsumami Shibori." Hand-pleated polyester shibori
17 "Sakuraso." Black velvet polyester and rayon with patterns of Echizen washi (Japanese paper)
75 "Trivet." Embroidered rendering on cotton of line-drawn wire racks, trivets, and other kitchenware
99 "Bamboo." White velvet polyester/rayon weave with a burn-out pattern of bamboo flowers

SHI-BO-RI JAPAN
76 Silk stitched shibori

エリックさんの新・和食
THE BREAKAWAY JAPANESE KITCHEN

2003年6月6日　第1刷発行

著　者　エリック・ガワー
発行者　畑野文夫
発行所　講談社インターナショナル株式会社
　　　　〒112-8652
　　　　東京都文京区音羽1-17-14
　　　　電話　03-3944-6493（編集部）
　　　　　　　03-3944-6492（営業部・業務部）
　　　　ホームページ www.kodansha-intl.co.jp

印刷所　大日本印刷株式会社
製本所　牧製本印刷株式会社